Re-Write Men

poems by

Michael Gaspeny

Finishing Line Press
Georgetown, Kentucky

Re-Write Men

Copyright © 2017 by Michael Gaspeny
ISBN 978-1-63534-355-7 First Edition
All rights reserved under International and Pan-American Copyright Conventions.
No part of this book may be reproduced in any manner whatsoever without written permission from the publisher, except in the case of brief quotations embodied in critical articles and reviews.

ACKNOWLEDGMENTS

With gratitude to the editors of the publications below. Some of these poems have undergone alterations.

Apogee: Elementary School
The Best of the Fuquay-Varina Reading Series, 2014: Crossing
Brilliant Corners: A Journal of Jazz and Literature: Undercurrent
Camel City Dispatch: William Beseeches Sister Rosetta
Flying South: Re-Write Man Transformed in Venice; Preacher Cruckshanks' Prophecy; The Strawberry
Iodine Poetry Journal: The Miracle Vacuum; de Chirico in Dixie
Kakalak: Vet at the Mall, Warren, Michigan; Chugging Lethe; Flipper at the Trees Motel
Kentucky Review: Hadassah's Property
The Lyricist: Process-Server
Naugatuck River Review: The Mojo Network; Saginaw Photo, 1968
O. Henry Magazine: Leashed
Opus: Take This Camel; The Bleeding Hearts of Redbud Lane; Memorial Stadium

Publisher: Leah Maines

Editor: Christen Kincaid

Cover Art: Lee Zacharias

Author Photo: Lee Zacharias

Cover Design: Elizabeth Maines McCleavy

Printed in the USA on acid-free paper.
Order online: www.finishinglinepress.com
also available on amazon.com

Author inquiries and mail orders:
Finishing Line Press
P. O. Box 1626
Georgetown, Kentucky 40324
U. S. A.

Table of Contents

Elementary School 1
Crossing 2
Chugging Lethe 3
The Miracle Vacuum 4
Preacher Cruckshanks' Prophecy 5
William Beseeches Sister Rosetta 6
What You Can't Say 7
The Mojo Network 8
Slits in the Furnace 9
Flipper at the Trees Motel 10
Take This Camel 11
The Bleeding Hearts of Redbud Lane 12
Leashed 13
Hadassah's Property 14
From the Plastic Pumpkin 17
Undercurrent 18
Chump Change 19
Process-Server 20
Memorial Stadium 21
Saginaw Photo, 1968 22
Vet at the Mall, Warren, Michigan 23
The Strawberry 24
de Chirico in Dixie 25
Re-Write Man Transformed in Venice 26

For Lee always

*Neon thanks to my pal Steve Cushman and poetry warriors
Donna Love Wallace, John Haugh, Sam Barbee,
and Angell Caudill*

*Joy to the Blumenthal family for the wonder of
Wildacres Retreat and the inspiration I've received from
my friends there*

Elementary School

After detention, I skyed a rock
to let off a little steam,
thrilled as it soared above
the glittering sidewalk.
Down the way, a blur of legs.
I yelled, a little boy fell,
papers floating from a notebook.

I ran to the clump at the curb,
begging God not to take him,
pressed a handkerchief to his bloody nape,
pleaded him to his senses, recovered
his papers, walked him home—
absorbed his mother's screaming.
That night I mistook the pounding wind
for cops coming to get me.

At church camp, I slammed my friend
against a wall for pulling down my shorts
in front of girls during a square-dance.
Bobby's skull thumped; his eyes dimmed;
he slid to the floor like a dummy.
The girls shrieked while I begged God
to kill me and spare Bobby.
A counselor's ammonia revived him.

Sixty years later, I still fear myself.
I don't need the Bible to show me Hell.
It's right here in my hands.

Crossing

Skeletal Stanley in flapping overalls skulked
behind the Cub Scouts at the school crossing. He cut
his legs with a razor blade and liked to show me
the swastikas in the gold hairs above his ankles.

After a rain, some boys crushed turtles
with a baseball bat. I wondered what the turtles
would have said if Aesop held a mic
to their last breath. *Why us?* I guessed.

Later that spring, Mom discovered my skin magazines.
She threw the temptresses in the trash with a splatter
of black-eyed peas, urged me to visit
our pastor's son Mark, leader of Teens for Jesus.

Mark bared something I couldn't tell Mom—
a jar with bull's balls floating in formaldehyde.
He swished the organs gently in the June light.

Because Mom could map every scratch in my room,
I wondered if the jar was allowed at the pastor's house.

Chugging Lethe

Fifty years after the delirium, I exalt
the boys who burned study lamps
instead of crushing cigarillos out on their palms.

Kudos to the straight arrows honoring the Honor Code
who never filched a test from a prof's desk or told
a best friend's girl, *There's nobody he can't leave.*

I praise the guys who refused to chug the night
like sloshing casks of Lethe and snore through the light
in sties where maggots teemed on chicken bones
in nests of festering clothes and crusted Trojans
shriveled under radiators.

Laurels to the sons who went home for holidays
and milked cows in freezing barns or shined
their fathers' cordovans for the sunrise service
instead of bursting through windshields.

If I could hold my Dad's steel-toed boots and whisk
the brush till a genie appeared, one wish would do.

The Miracle Vacuum

Then it was easy to mock the salesmen with the shakes
rumbling the Miracle anthem to the tune of *Power in the Blood*
to start the daily sales parley, Camels treading their lungs.
They endured the manager's snarling homily to receive
the free lunch card for Swiss steak at the bowling alley,
razor-nicked jaws above the counter gnawing and smoking,
one sale ahead of extinction, facing an afternoon of cold calls.

But sometimes a hot call came, and we threw darts
to seal the deal and pocket the fat commission. Then steady-handed,
these frog-eyed earls of Norfolk's boarding houses grazed
one another's feathers, three darts whizzing inside the bull's eye
while my ricocheting toss clattered to the floor,
raising hacking laughter.

Now the old crew has tottered down the alley
and guttered; the Miracle's enshrined in the Home Care
Hall of Fame; and it's hard to scoff
from my sleeping bag in a squat
where a previous occupant spray-painted
I've Got Guts! on the liver-spotted ceiling.

I, the Miracle's chastened Homer, recite the ancestral names—
wreathing each in a smoke ring—heir to the family fortune.

Preacher Cruckshanks' Prophecy

The dying preacher said he liked me
because I knew the street where God
had flung him down and he'd turned his liquor house
into the Church of the Holy Ground.
A lion of the Lord, he was down to bones and a roar.

I was sent to the hospital to soothe Preacher Cruckshanks
because God prodded him from under the wall TV
where I muted *The Price is Right*.
When pain struck, he yelled and squeezed my hand
till the spasms stopped. *Jesus sent you*, he intoned.
I was glad to please him but knew my limitations.

One day I mentioned Paul's conversion
outside Damascus and asked the preacher
to tell me more about the morning God grabbed him.
He hollered, *Why do you keep binding my hands
and hauling me back there? I won't be your convict! Go!*
Stunned, I apologized and left, resolving to let him lead me.

Next visit he smiled, patted my hand,
made me promise to leave it *right there*
on the rail. He drifted off. When his cheeks puffed,
I flexed my aching fingers. He shot awake and wailed,
*I told you not to move your hand! Why won't you listen?
God has told me how you'll end. But I won't speak it unless
He makes me.* I forced my fingers back to the rail.

Soon the gasps began. The preacher shot awake, grabbing
my hand. He shook like I was frying him, and bellowed:
Get out! You're hell-bound! Out!
I wanted to shout: *Then you can marry me
and the Devil's daughter!* But I hadn't come
to scorn the demented. I left, curses hissing in my head.

The preacher died next morning.
One day I'll learn if he told my fortune.

William Beseeches Sister Rosetta

This morning I need
your sun in my marrow
as you wheel the diseased
into the dining hall for prayer.
The fat cats phased you out.

When you clasped my shoulders,
my soul slid to your feet like a dog.
I swear we stayed alive
to hear you call our names
one more time—*William!*
Mother Moten! Mrs. Pontheola Jones!...
You made us sound like revelations.

My longing swells in the empty dining hall.
March wind thrashes the scrubwoods
behind the dumpster. Whumps the windows.
Twirls the hems of the thinning tablecloths.

The stumps stir inside my robe.
Now, Sister! Tell us how beautiful we are.
Make us love ourselves and one another.
Pray it like you did, Sweet Rosetta!

What You Can't Say

The nurse came to treat Mojo's legs.
She asked me to leave, but he said,
*No! I want him to see what that shotgun done,
and I didn't do what that boy's brothers said!*

The nurse broke the scabs; the punctures ran.
He didn't groan. The legs were numb.
But when she treated the sore burrowing
into his hip, he clawed the bed.

The nurse left. A sweet stink stayed.
Mojo saw my dread and swore:
I won't let them cut off my legs!
I said, *Then I'll miss you.*

He twiddled junk mail choked in a drawer,
vowing, *These certified checks will keep my sister
for life. I'll visit Thanksgivings. You come for dinner.*

Sure, Jo, I said, picturing that glorious meal,
turkey-shaped manna, all wounds healed.

The Mojo Network

Mojo was in the game when a shotgun blast
ruined his legs and addled his brain,
but to the end, he memorized *Bonanza*
and praised the Cartwrights as if they were holy,
warning villains: *Oh, Lord! Wait till Ben finds out!*
Once, after I asked him to catch me up on the plot,
he said, *Watch the horses! The real show's inside.*

His words came on like ganja in my mind.
Manes shined in the silver Western light.
What were the horses' names? No two alike.
Who brought the basin to the room above the saloon?
Did she and her lover roll in the dust under the studio moon?
If the buckboard were a telegraph, what did it creak?
That Mojo network took me deep.

A few visits later, an Ensure dripped from his tray to the floor.
Oprah replaced Little Joe. Mojo's eyes were tuned inside.

Across from the Hubbard Family Funeral Home,
men passed a bottle in a muddy lot
and fed palette scraps to a flaming barrel.
I squeezed into a pew, pressed by a vision:
Behind the gleaming skyline,
pilgrims slumped from the projects
to the fire to the chapel, where Mojo
briefly reigned before cremation.

Afterward, Mr. Hezikiah Hubbard, distributing
brochures, said, *We're always here for you.*
In the street, old times rode the wind.
Mojo howled, *See out the blinds? They come to kill me!*

Slits in the Furnace

Les Hillis was a drifter with bloody phlegm and a DNR notice
over his bed, but he swaggered like a golden-robed welterweight
through the creeping maze of his firetrap hotel.

All that spring, we bought used books and sunned
in the city gardens. The first hot noon, we joked about snow,
so I asked what he wanted for Christmas. *The road*, he said.
And I'm gonna get it! That night, Saint Nick came.
Les's westerns blazed behind the lobby desk, but the manager,
heeding Les's will, refused to tell the location of his ashes.
Nowhere for a farewell.

Les leads me through alleys, laughing, spitting.
He grins at rats gnawing pepperoni in a dumpster.
A meat problem, he scoffs, jerking me to his face. *I'll be back,
but I ain't Christ.* His brawler's glare splits my brain.
He struts from his cinders.

Flipper at the Trees Motel

Gold-tipped leaves fly in the last wisps of sun,
alight on drive-in crack and thigh trade,
tick my neck as I knock at room 29,
$200 a month, no maid service.

A tin bucket clinks as Flipper mops
his bathroom floor. I've seen this chore.
His lank hair swings. He stoops and staggers.
A Pall Mall smolders in a tin ashtray.
Cancer spreads lungs to spine.
He works lefthanded, right arm dangling.

He coughs and stumbles to the door,
shirks help with his camouflage jacket.
He wants a cell phone.
At what he calls *Val-Mark*, the clerk flirts
with the auto mechanic behind us.
We were here first, I say.
She says, *He can't die in the store.*
I want to get in her face, but he tugs my sleeve.

Back in nicotine-coated 29, he wants to eat,
though he can barely breathe, says,
Please get me some pintos, cornbread, slaw.
Bringing the cartons, I tell him, *It's on me.*
He squints at the stapled tab on the bag.
His fingers twitch inside the left pants pocket
where he lives. He claws out oddments,
including a carrot bobber with a yellow top
from our fishing last spring.

He palms me a five, a dime and penny, says,
*Thanks for taking me to Val-Mark. Don't get shot
in the parking lot. Don't get laid. Be faithful to your wife.*
I say, *OK,* then lean in close and ask the daily question:
Listen, Flipper, isn't there somebody you want me to call?

Take This Camel

> *—It is easier for a camel to go through the eye of a needle, than for a rich person to enter the kingdom of heaven. (Matthew 19:24)*

When you labeled the nurse's aide
the girl who does the room,
I almost scolded, *Her name's LaDonna.*
She dresses your cancer sores and eases you
into your cherished ensembles.
I recalled the fate of the camel.

Then you had me feel the dent
in your skull from a silver table lighter
an enraged boy hurled off a verandah
because you fetched your brother to lunch,
ending their fun. You could have died.

If Matthew's true, you'd bleed again
from grinding against the needle.
I saw the eye taunting you.

You might twist your right arm through
but never the useless left, yellow-blue.
When you were eight, a stroke confined your father,
the biggest banker in Savannah, to a private hospital
for three years. The day he came home, a flying boy
bowled you down Day School stairs. You staggered
to the house, holding the shattered arm and dropped
at your father's wheelchair. He died reaching out.

Seventy years later, you cried, *Daddy, wait!*
When the sheets stopped shaking, I wanted to raise you and beg.

The Bleeding Hearts of Redbud Lane

When Anita Hill and Clarence Thomas were at war,
you yelled: *I love seeing darkies at each other's throats!*
because I had friends whose color differed from yours.
You limped merrily up your driveway, World War II vet,
shrapnel in your legs, American Aryan of Redbud Lane.

You walked your beagle Reb three times a day till cancer
sapped him. You said wasting away was a fitting fate
for pointy-headed liberals like me, but a good dog deserved
to run forever. As Reb faded, a creature invaded your kitchen
each night during a drought. It drank Reb's water
and slipped out. *What is it? How does it get in?* you asked.
I lied when I promised to think about it.

That fall, I ignored the wonder in your voice
as you occupied my porch at dusk. I kept my briefcase
between you and the door. Once, you asked me to hold
the jar containing Reb's ashes. I did to get rid of you.
You slumped across the street as if you'd been stabbed.

In a Thanksgiving storm, a flying limb webbed the windshield
of your Chevy. When you didn't come out, I found
you dead, propped in bed, one ear cocked
toward the kitchen where Reb's bowl still brimmed.

You bled to save hatred and wish me dead.
I savored my contempt. What if I'd said,
Let me crawl under the house?

Leashed

We find a sweet, russet-colored hound
on our morning walk. You give her
that loving Black Lab nuzzle while I examine
her tags. Name: Penny, no address.
We press the bells on Wentworth Way
till Penny's recognized by a brisk woman with a cell.
She makes a call. Her yapping terrier rakes the screen.
You're stunned anew by the hostility of your fellows.
Behind your back, across the street,
Penny slips inside a door.

You turn to bewildering absence, tug sniffing
up three walkways before Penny's image dissolves,
I'd like to think, in a shower of copper dust
beneath a cartoon magician's wand—Plink!—
and her smell slides into your bank of scents.
You pick up the pace. If only I could learn the same.

Hadassah's Property

1. A Little Detergent

Before you went to the Hebrew home,
husband in the ground, losing your mind,
you begged me for help in mailing
a mini-box of Tide containing two pebbles
of soap to Merlina, a teenaged friend in Athens
who'd gone up the chimney at Auschwitz
along with all your family
after Hitler strangled Greece.
Had you forgotten she was ash
or did you hope detergent could bring her back?
The ads did promise miracles.

We couldn't mail the soap,
not even to the North Pole.
The cellophane tape you applied thirty years ago
was peeling and car wash coupons
made insufficient postage. You were shrieking
in Greek. Holding you, I promised to handle the details.
This air-mail facsimile is the best I can do,
requesting confirmation of delivery.

2. A Pool of Shadows

Once, a photo of your family picnicking
appeared in the *Morning Star*—
forty or so souls and you
with a circle around your head
identifying the only survivor.
What it must have cost to wear!

You told me you lurched awake each night,
sure your mother lay downstairs
on the carpet below the menorah.
You always tried to hug the shadows
whose emptiness made you gasp.
In August, the carpet throbbed like a fever.
What if your yearning came true
and she'd been there breathing—
twenty-five years younger than her daughter?
How could you explain?

3. *A Ruined Arbor*

In sunny weather, you and beloved Nikos lounged
under backyard maples at a wrought-iron table
bordered by day lilies, shaded by an umbrella.
With your matching blue numbers in the buttery light,
Nikos told the same death-camp stories
as if you'd never heard them and hadn't been there,
as if, told often enough, they might shatter. You begged
him to stop, feeling the other neighbors edge farther away.
Even so, for you both, joy was this arbor.

Now the table rusts; the umbrella has burst;
the undergrowth has eaten your flowers.
Wisteria wreathes the bower.
A few years before you left,
the jungle took the yard.
You refused my help.

4. A Throne

One April morning, you and Nikos strolled
down the street, each holding an arm
of a lawn chair plucked from a neighbor's refuse.
The backrest was shredded, exposing aluminum ribs.
The find disappeared inside the garage till Nikos died.
Then you placed the chair among gray leaves
at the back fence facing your kitchen window.
Its hungry look chilled me until the metal blazed
in dusk's glare. You had chosen the spot with care.
I saw Nikos ruling there.

A few years later, kudzu choked the chair
and sealed your back door.
You didn't speak of Nikos anymore.

5. An Accusation

So many autumns after Nikos died,
we raked leaves in our front yards,
teasing back and forth to make time fly:
You're invited to the Leaf-Rakers' Ball, I called.
You replied, *No, my friend, the band plays here. Come dance!*
This morning, as I raked, your echo drove me
to an accusation you had too much faith to make—
If God cannot deliver the soap,
spin shadows into your mother,
place you and Nikos on a throne
crowned by an arbor of stars,
then what was any breathing for,
most of all, first breath, first tide?

From the Plastic Pumpkin

June breeze jiggles your old porch swing
above the crusted birdbath and ragged grass
where you blistered on a chaise
in heart-shaped shades, dreaming of stardom.
Three summers since you and your mom left town.

That last Halloween, too old for the game,
you rang my bell in blond wig and beauty mark,
identifying yourself as Marilyn Monroe.
I doled you a Kit Kat like the ten-year-olds.

The time you baby-sat for my son,
you and a chum ate the whole pizza
except the scrap you granted him.
You said, *I hope you'll have me back.*
That's why I'm writing.

From the plastic pumpkin of amends,
please accept my apology
for condescension
and know your love for your mom
flourishes along with the purple-leaf plum.
You bloomed next to her on a Tweety Bird blanket,
planting impatiens. Arranging wickets for croquet,
you sprang to her directions. Winning, you curtsied.

The tiles you two laid along the driveway live on.
My favorite has the gold key in the blue heart.
The legend reads: *Magic is believing. Belief is in the heart.*
The heart holds the key. The key unlocks the door.
I owe you, Friend. Sometimes it opens me.

Undercurrent

in memory of Bill Evans

Strange resting-place for Dreamy Bill—
Rose Lawn, Baton Rouge,
near the Mississippi's turgid stew.
Far from glasses chiming at the Vanguard,
the enthralled Parisians, the Danish boy hiding
under the piano to touch your trouser cuffs.

Among gluttons slain by crawfish etouffee,
you, who fed malnutrition like a lap dog, lie
next to older brother Harry, who chose the pistol.
In Louisiana, you saw *an inexplicable indifference
about the way people face existence.*
It takes an Onegin to know one.

On early album covers, you look spellbound
by music or junk or both, practicing
six hours a day, drifting from Rachmaninoff
into the bay of your soul. Though handsome
and athletic, enamored of golf and dice,
you'd pass for a philatelist living with Mother.
Myshkin-ite, you made humility a vice.

When a needle paralyzed your left arm, you played
a week-long engagement right-handed.
For decades, Doctor Bulgakov reserved a table
near the stage and took your vital signs, amazed
by the doppelganger drumming inside your temples.
Near the end, friends say you played your soul.

Fifty-one—how did you survive yourself that long?
In Manhattan, your head reached the keys.
Then: booking in the Sportsman's Paradise.

Chump Change

I listened to *The Quest* twice last night,
strange album you willed me. My ears swept
the spheres for your voice as your grit mixed
with the cherry blossoms in the Potomac.
Mal Waldron, Booker Ervin, Eric Dolphy,
Ron Carter, fierce players for a fade-out—
coins sprinkling from your pockets
as you grope for your pants in the dark;
a kiss to stifle my murmurs; change
on the morning carpet for me to pick up.

You taught me jazz but never got to Waldron,
forevered by O'Hara in *The Day Lady Died*—
Billie whispered a song along the keyboard to Mal Waldron.
Such an urbane name! Has he shown you the town?
I see you spinning vinyl at the Galaxy Lounge,
arms around new chums while I scratch my back
against hearts gouged in our booth
at the Last Round. How many have held on?

Hush those fools. Ring my cell. Slip me some sound.
Say, *This one's dedicated to an old chump monking
around The Capital of the Unfree World.*
Play 'Alone Together.'

Process-Server

Outside Holy Trinity, last Sunday, Sally Sleigh told us,
Scott's gone back to family connections in Maine.
My wife Julia asked, *Which Scott?* I was ashamed.
Not so long ago, he graced our circle.

Racquetball king, mixer of a matchless martini,
Scott could drive a golf ball from Charlotte to Miami.
How the ladies loved to jitterbug with that hunk!
But his shoulder poke and grainy voice counted most.

Three years past, money middling, wife disinclined
to work, bright son deserving Day School education,
Scott left the insurance game for a brokerage firm
a microbrew before the market plunge.

He declined invitations, offered none.
It's been six months, Julia huffed.
I said, *Give him time. It's pride.*
She replied, *Membership has obligations.*
In due course, she saw he was dropped.
Was he as sick of us all as I was?

Last fall in the park, I pretended not to see Scott
tossing a football with his son until his call
caught me. Surely he translated the fake cheer
I flung over my shoulder as I trudged on.
My tone stuck in my ears, too sham for even me to stand.

I wanted to jog back, snatch the ball, and yell,
Go long, son! When my pass wobbled in the grass,
I'd exclaim, *This old arm could use some oil!*
Then we'd all laugh.

I asked the sky why I was here. Ezekiel did not appear.

Memorial Stadium

For ten summers Stub left the farm at 6 p.m. and blazed
forty miles from Leaksville to Greensboro for the Bats' games—
sheepish pope of the stands above first, dome-shaped head
enshrining *The Baseball Encyclopedia*.

So, when Stub stopped coming, we were puzzled
and hurt. Had drought sapped him, or the scrape of the latch
on his bedroom door, wife shutting him out?
We all knew the couch and floor. I followed the obits
from Leaksville—nothing. It took a season
to elevate Stub to the pantheon of our nostalgia.

I swear I saw him last night in our old spot,
but I had no one to elbow. Four or five years had passed
fast as the Amtrak whizzing beyond the flagpole.
Fans had abandoned the crumbling stadium. Rooster Man,
Choir Boy, Tom the Bomb, all gone, even Mr. Lens,
giving kids their photos, and Suds, who lived so close by,
when he whistled, his beagle howled.

I drank beer in the empty bleachers beyond third.
As I mused about Stub, a vision of the Colosseum splattered
my daze. After the gladiators slaughtered the beasts,
the hackers split the carcasses, heaped the gore in baskets,
and slung the meat to the rabble at the gates.

I jerked from my trance. Stub had gone. I stank like a butcher's bucket.
Resisting the beer man's call, I dragged my remains from the park.

Saginaw Photo, 1968

There's Robbie. Pa has posed him in the grass.
He's about six, hair on end because there's a big blow
off the bay or he senses what's ahead.
The claws of that tomcat in his lap are cutting
his thighs, but Pa has snarled, *You better smile!*

Ten years later, in a flare-up over the last piece
of cherry pie, Pa jabbed a fork in Robbie's side.
A train rattled by. Robbie flipped Pa off the porch,
ass over suspenders, and raced to the rails.

At Pa's howl, frogs burst out of ditches;
ticks streamed off the dogs; a cloud of gnats
swarmed Robbie as he swung into a boxcar.
There must have been idle hands in hell
that noon to plague a bony, tongue-tied boy.
Afterward, Robbie's brows always twitched.

For forty years, he stocked groceries in Wisconsin,
Packers cap jerked over his eyes. When customers
asked for mustard, the brim replied, *Aisle Five.*
Behind his back, bagboys called him *The Insect.*
His solution: lakes of Miller High Life, fields of Lucky Strikes.

When X-rays showed spots on his lungs, he traded the ice
for a rusty trailer in a co-op down in Sorrento, Florida.
At the Snowbird Tap Room, he heard a blow-hard say, *Hop-stop!*
Hop-stop! He's wired like a squirrel. Then booming laughter.
Robbie squirmed into a sleeping bag, applied a .38 to his head.

He left this picture and five twenties in an envelope marked *EMS.*

Vet at the Mall, Warren, Michigan

We scavenge the vast parking lot at dawn.
I grant the gulls Happy Meal scraps.
I want a glance from the *Free Press* babe
slinging papers in condos beyond.
There was a time she might have turned.

My mojo's blowing in Iraq.
Once I was an acolyte, second-string tackle
at Loyola High, part-timer at White Castle.
The Towers crashed; I fell for the weapons
of mass destruction. I discovered myself.

Warning barrels glare around
caved-in asphalt, gouged by Detroit winters.
At Tikret, I took a picture of Saddam's monument
beheaded in the rubble, good for a free buzz
in 12 Mile Road taprooms for six months.

I cast my meds to the winds. Mom changed the locks.
My lady got a restraining order. Loaded at the Amvet,
I karaoked *My Way*, gave a wife a little squeeze.
She asked me outside, clipped my jaw, dropped me
in the gravel, yelling, *Semper Fi, Dawg!*

A vacant store takes my snapshot—a throat
below a Tigers cap, sack of cash-in empties on my back.
I chime and clack toward Farmer Jack's. My last interviewer
asked, *Where do you see yourself in ten years?*
      I was dumbstruck.

Now I'd say, *In an asphalt crater, wearing a suit of gulls.*

The Strawberry

As I rose from the chair, my head sloshed.
Dostoevsky splashed on the carpet. Drunk
without a drop, I hugged furniture, staggered
to the stairs, my lame Black Lab Ollie underfoot.
To keep from crashing on him, I crawled up to bed.

The mattress pitched with stroke-wracked patients
I'd visited as a volunteer: Polly swelling in bed
like a fiend's experiment. Not so long ago,
her horseshoes rang the stake…Willie took heart
from *Raiders of the Lost Ark* novels I read him.
When an orderly brought the lifting machine,
he flung the man across the room….
Lonnie, face and arms all that moved,
a scale of grunts for diction. Yet he smiled
and spread his hands like he was singing….
Where would I find their courage?

Morning! Ollie nudged me to go out.
I teetered downstairs after the limping dog.
At the back door, crows plucked a putrefying possum.
Out front, rush hour. I leashed Ollie.
Fixated drivers whizzed by, thumbing devices.
The nails of Ollie's trick leg scratched on the pavement.
The wind pounded us. Any time, he could topple.
In the stubble at the curb, a dandelion.
The sun struck purple blooms against a dingy house.
I almost dropped from beauty. I cooed, *Oh, look, Sweet Boy!*

He cocked a leg. Traffic cleared. I saw the man
in the Buddhist parable being chased by a tiger
toward a cliff, where a strawberry dangles on a vine.
Stripes growl among the rocks below. Today, the fragrance.
Tomorrow, the berry spurting under my tongue, as I swing out.

de Chirico in Dixie

The master of melancholy would find inspiration here
in the sun-stunned back yards of Rolling Hills,
where basketballs shrivel on cracked concrete
under rusty rims. Picnic tables wither.
Ivy snakes through the mortar of stone barbecue pits.
Garages contain burial mounds of sports debris
until the equipment rebels…

Cadres of putters, oars, boomerangs, Louisville Sluggers
drive kids into layup drills, couples to croquet, the little ones
to *Mother May I?* governed by bossy sitters.
The four o'clock whistle summons beach umbrellas and board games
till reading hour. Tents are raised. Around the campfire,
hot dogs on coat hangers, s'mores, and ghost stories.
Connubial dancing's enforced to *In the Still of the Night*
on the turntable. But with couples cheek-to-cheek,
kids at hide-and-seek, a father, screened by labradoodles,
crawls toward his smartphone. Soon the revolt is crushed,
captured by the TV trucks.

In Indian summer
a new girl from Montana
rolls a hoop down the street at dusk,
triggering flashing sensors,
eyeballs at replacement windows,
while dogs on their hind legs moan and claw
at invisible fences.

Re-Write Man Transformed in Venice

1
I clarified garble, killed clichés, bridged gaps,
commanded facts like a cop directing traffic.
I was the story I couldn't revise.

I fathered the child Charlotte wanted to warm a stricken house,
in part replicating the meticulous man she hated.
We had married to escape ourselves. When she slashed
her wrists, she pleaded, *Let me die.*
I used my regimental-striped ties for tourniquets.

Our son David numbed into an Eagle Scout
on permanent retreat. Charlotte pursued art history.
Jack Daniels and trysting professors kept her pet threat
from the paper: *Reporter's Wife Plunges from* Herald
Parking Deck. Scorn for me and bourbon killed her.

2
Tonight I stroll the moonlit streets past bungalows
where young families sleep, weary from weekends at the beach.
Last of the old cast, I cross the driveway where a stroke
finished Mrs. Hinds, who had the addict son. One howling night,
she called to borrow a can of soup, explaining:
I'm broke, and Lloyd stripped the pantry.
What did it say about her days that she appealed
to a near-stranger? I stuffed a bag with food, tucked
some bills inside. Her terrier Sparky sprang at the screen.
Mrs. Hinds avoided my eyes.

Nine Marches later, I found her dead in the rain,
clasping *The Penny Saver.* Shielding her
with my umbrella, I dialed 911, then recited what prayers
I could remember. Arthritic Sparky whimpered
at the fence. I entered the house and let him in.

Skeletal Lloyd snored on the couch, crack-pipe in his lap.
The cold of that home made me thankful for my own.
There's always worse.

I know that Tudor house on the hill down to the knobs,
having searched for a suicidal widower after pleas
from his long-distance daughter. Calling *Roland, are you there?*
I opened every door. In the attic, I checked
the rafters for something dangling, then found Roland
hoisting a mug in the sports bar at the corner.
I staggered home.

There's more pain on Redbud Lane,
but tonight I bow to the moon.

        3
No one's ever free. Yet I feel released
from my weakness and the wraiths of this street.
Last May, retired, I found the appetite
to sop up Italy. Oh, blustery Venezia, in a square
where headlines climbed cathedral stairs
and festive voices sailed from the five-star hotels
across the Grand Canal, the sea-winds tore off
the festering lapels of my self-pity. My lungs swelled
like a gondolier's. I howled with the gale.
        For now, I have been rewritten.

As a poet, short story writer, and reporter, **Michael Gaspeny** has published widely. For nearly four decades, he taught English and Journalism, mainly at Bennett College and High Point University, where he received the distinguished teaching award. While gaining an M.F.A. in creative writing at the University of Arkansas, he worked as a sportswriter covering the Razorbacks and as a general assignments reporter. His features on Bill Clinton's first campaign for national office have been frequently quoted in biographies of the former president. Gaspeny holds an M.A. from the University of Richmond and an undergraduate degree from Randolph-Macon College.

He lives in Greensboro, North Carolina with his wife Lee Zacharias, the novelist and essayist. They have two sons.

www.ingramcontent.com/pod-product-compliance
Lightning Source LLC
LaVergne TN
LVHW041513070426
835507LV00012B/1536